Letter from the Editors

These articles were very popular when we originally posted them a few years ago on Anglotopia. So, we were very excited to update them a bit and find some beautiful images that we didn't have to share the first time.

This is hopefully the first of many special issues we will put out every few months focusing on beautiful bits of Britain we think are worth sharing with everyone.

We hope you enjoy this exploration of Britain 10 most beautiful gardens.

Happy reading!

Cheers,
Jonathan & Jackie
Anglotopia

Table of Co

About the Magazine

The Great Gardens Special was published by Anglotopia LLC, a USA registered Corporation. All contents copyrighted and may not be reproduced without permission.

Letters to the Editors may be addressed to:

Anglotopia LLC
1101 Cumberland Crossing #120
Valparaiso, IN 46383
USA

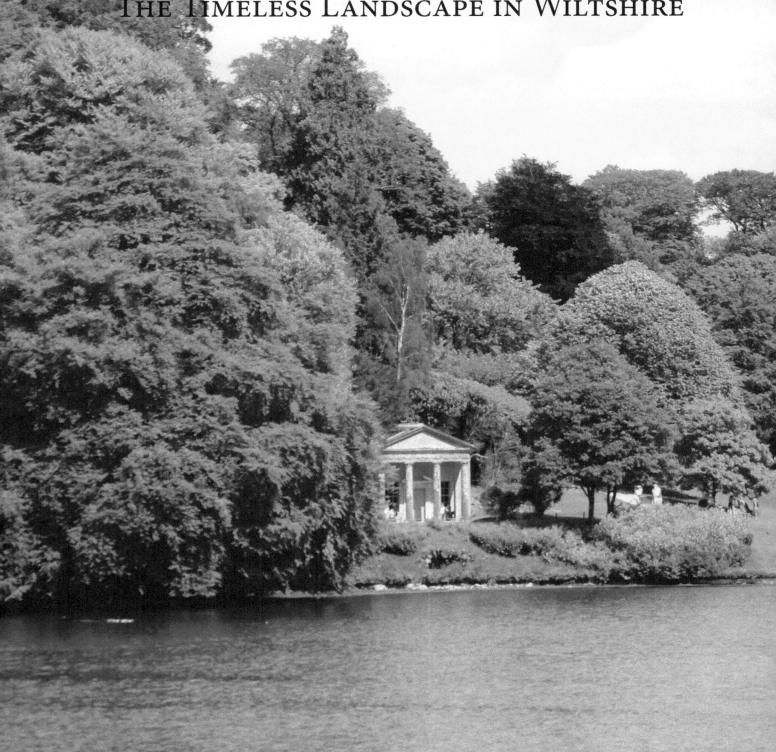

STOURHEAD

THE TIMELESS LANDSCAPE IN WILTSHIRE

Stourhead is a large landscape garden in Wiltshire, built in the 18th century. It epitomizes the Picturesque style of garden design. It has a large lake with numerous classical-style features and Italianate buildings dotted around it. The garden is a beautiful walk at all seasons along winding pathways through trees and with various views across the lake.

The Story of Stourhead

Many of the estates of the British aristocracy are worlds unto themselves. The Stourhead estate is no exception. Totalling 2,650 acres, the estate includes a Palladian Manor House, a village called Stourton, woodlands, farms and a garden. The estate is located at the source of the river Stour, in Wiltshire and was the property of the Barons of Stourton from the 13th century until 1714, when the estate was sold to the Hoare family, who were wealthy bankers. The estate remained in the family until it was transferred to the National Trust in 1946.

Shortly after acquiring the estate Henry Hoare I had the original manor house torn down and replace with a house designed in the Palladian style that was in vogue at that time. The new Manor House was completed in 1725 and became a repository for the family's library and art collection for the next 200 years. Henry Hoare II inherited the property and having spent time in Europe taking the Grand Tour - an extended trip around Europe that was part of a young gentleman's education - he was inspired to construct a revolutionary garden based on the French and Italian landscapes he had seen, and especially on the representations of these gardens seen in landscape paintings.

Prior to this time, most gardens were designed on the principles established during the Renaissance, which emphasised geometry and straight lines. This was particularly apparent in the use of vistas. These were long sight-lines consisting of grass flanked by trees. The trees were often clipped into hedges, and the lawn areas could be used for riding or festivities. Where sight-lines intersected, there would usually be a pond, fountain, statue or obelisk to mark that point and to be visible along the vistas. Closer to houses these vistas gave way to square or rectangular areas decorated with ornate designs in clipped plants or coloured gravels, called parterres. Planting was restricted, and more interesting plants were grown in pots and arranged along the various terraces and walkways. The goal was to impose a precise geometry on the natural landscape and carry out the task assigned to Man by God, the perfection of an imperfect world.

By the early 18th century this approach had degenerated into more and more grandiose designs, with endless vistas and enormous parterres requiring armies of gardeners. The time was ripe for a change, and it was in England that this change happened.

Alexander Pope, who was born in 1688, is usually remembered as a poet, but he was also an avid gardener and had an estate at Twickenham. He was the first to preach a new approach to gardening, which involved balance, not simple symmetry; relative modesty, not ostentation; and most revolutionary of all, curves, not just straight lines. This idea was indeed revolutionary after the dominance of geometry for so long. In one poem he also wrote, "let Nature never be forgot, consult the Genius of the Place in all." In other words, he said that the character of the site should be respected and incorporated into the design, not obliterated under geometry. A garden should contain natural features that expressed nature, rather than suppressed it.

Pope had a gardener called William Kent, who looked to art for inspiration and was inspired by the dramatic paintings of natural landscapes that were popular at the time. This meant ending the domination of the straight line and the need, as another poet of the time put it, to "show to the pupils of Design, the triumphs of the Waving Line." This was a deeply radical idea in a way that can be hard to grasp today. The use of curves and rounded contours became the style known as the English Landscape Garden. Since an important goal was to create pictures that were viewed from various vantage points, it is often also called the Picturesque. Historians have noted that women were beginning to play a more important part in society and male views were being tempered and softened by the introduction of more feminine principles, leading to a softening of the hard edges of earlier landscapes.

William Kent went on to design a number of significant gardens, but although he never worked at Stourhead, the garden there is the epitome of the Picturesque style. Starting around 1742 and working with the architect Henry Flitcroft, Henry Hoare built a garden almost unique for the time, which created a

series of landscape views decorated with ornamental buildings and varying as one walked through the garden – a private Grand Tour in fact.

The Garden

The heart of Stourhead is The Lake, which was created by damming a small stream behind the village of Stourton, which, with the waters also flowing in from the springs that are the source of the river Stour, flooded a small valley. The earthen dam and overflow can be seen at the end of the lake. A pathway runs around the lake, approaching or moving away from it to reveal a series of views, each one different, from several vantage points. The garden is inward-looking and makes little use of the wider landscape beyond. It was designed as a complete internal experience, to stimulate memory, reflection, and musings on philosophy and life.

The only plant material used was trees. By skilful planting of groups and clumps of woodland, views are alternately hidden and then suddenly revealed, creating a series of surprises as the views unfold while moving around the lake. This element of surprise creates a sense of narrative or sequence to

the trip around the lake, which would have been on foot, horseback or carriage, depending on the season, weather and the occasion.

In the early 19th century plantings of rhododendron, azalea, laurel and other flowering shrubs were added by Hoare's grand-son and when these were in bloom they became a feature of the garden. Towards the end of the 20th century, accompanied by considerable controversy, most of these later plantings were removed to restore the original appearance and views of Hoare's design.

The walk around the lake is 1½ to 2 miles long, depending on exactly what route is taken. Hoare's intent was to create a series of pictures featuring various buildings in the classic style, reminiscent of his trip around Italy. Flitcroft designed several buildings in the style of temples: The Temple of Ceres, built in 1744; the Temple of Hercules and a smaller-scale copy of the Pantheon in Rome, added in 1754; and the Temple of Apollo in 1765. Inside these temples, there are various statues of classic figures such as Hercules and Flora. Latin inscriptions are often placed over the entrances. Mastery of Latin and Greek and a detailed knowledge of the classics and of mythology were the main education of a gentleman.

On the far-side of the lake from the house, a dark pathway leads to a Grotto area, with two caves containing statues and pools. Grottos were a popular garden feature at the time, and Alexander Pope also had one in his garden. These were representations of the underworld, or of the unconscious, as well as being cool, shady places to retreat to on hot summer days.

Other features include the Bristol High Cross - a gothic spire brought to the garden from the city of Bristol, an Obelisk and the Gothic Cottage or Hermitage. This is a small stone cottage often found in other gardens of the period. Some owners went so far as to hire someone to live in isolation in their Hermitage, as a hermit, to add a frisson to the garden tour. It does not appear that Hoare did so.

In the course of renovation, many landowners swept away the villages on their estates or moved them out of sight. At Stourhead the village of Stourton was retained, with some beautification, as a visible feature. Other later additions were the Palladian Bridge at one end of the lake and Alfred's Tower on a nearby hill, where legend had it that in 879 the Saxon King Alfred the Great, had camped before defeating the Danes and uniting the British tribes.

Influences

Stourhead was followed by a fashion for the Landscape Garden that swept England. Its main practitioner was Lancelot "Capability" Brown who developed a formula for what were referred to as Improvements and whose style became the only approach to informality possible. He converted hundreds of estates and created much of the 'look' of large English gardens.

Because Stourhead was such a self-contained world, with its features and activities, it has also been proposed as the proto-type of the contemporary Theme Park.

As Seen In...

- Pride and Prejudice (2005)
- Barry Lyndon (1975)
- Miss Marple: Nemesis (1987)

Further Reading

- Stourhead Landscape Garden, by Oliver Garnett (2000). This is the National Trust guidebook.
- Landscape and Antiquity: Aspects of English Culture at Stourhead 1718 to 1838, by K. Woodbridge (1970).
- Stourhead is also discussed in numerous books on the history of gardens and landscaping.

Practical Information

Stourhead Garden is near Mere, Wiltshire. Mere is a small town east of Glastonbury and a little south of the town of Warminster.

The gardens are open every day of the year, including all holidays, except for December 25th. Consult the National Trust for opening-hours each day, which vary with the seasons.

STOWE

One of the First Managed Landscape Gardens in England

Stowe is a grand estate in the Vale of Aylesbury north of London. It contains a large mansion and extensive grounds in the Landscape style, which developed during the 18th century in Georgian England to reflect a growing interest in an idealized natural landscape. This style uses informal views incorporating neo-classical temples and other structures in arrangements influenced by landscape paintings.

The Story

The estate of Stowe, in the attractive agricultural area of Aylesbury Vale, was owned from the late 16th century by the Temple family, who made their fortune from sheep farming in the Vale. Beginning around 1716, chiefly while Sir Richard Temple, the Viscount Cobham, owned the property up until 1846 when the family fortune ran out, a grand house and surrounding garden were built, much of which can still be seen today. The house, with a main frontage almost 1,000 feet long, was the scene of many grand events of Georgian England and is now Stowe School, a British public (i.e. independent fee-paying) school.

The work on the gardens was done by several of the most influential garden designers of the 17th century in the new Landscape style. This was a break with earlier formal styles which when done on a grand scale chiefly consisted of long, straight vistas of grass flanked by trees and marked by fountains, obelisks and other features where these vistas intersected.

Influenced by travels in Europe and a fashion for Greek and Roman mythology and classical architecture, gardens were opened up and most of the straight lines were removed, to be replaced by rolling hills and valleys dotted with informal clumps of trees. The geometrically organized formal gardens closer to the houses were replaced with grass terraces with views across the gardens or into the surrounding countryside. The goal was to create an idealized natural landscape, dotted with architectural features such as temples, in a style variously referred to as Picturesque, Arcadian or jardin anglais.

In 1716 Viscount Cobham hired the garden designer Charles Bridgeman to create new gardens around the extensions he was making to the existing mansion. Bridgeman came from obscure beginnings as a gardener to later rise to the position of Royal Gardener and his work at Stowe was an early part of his career modernising the estates of the nobility. His work at Stowe was transitional – he still clung to the geometry of straight lines and constructed several long walks lined with elms, chestnut trees or lime trees, but between them, he developed 'wilderness' with informal groups of trees and natural contours. He built lakes and ponds as well as amphitheatres and temples.

One of his great inventions was the ha-ha. A difficulty in opening up the landscape was the need to remove hedges and fences. Since there were no lawnmowers at that time grazing animals, especially sheep, were used to maintain the large grass areas. Some method was needed to keep these sheep and also deer away from the house itself, and the ha-ha was a concealed ditch that could not be seen from important vantage points but which stopped animals approaching the house. The ha-ha became an important necessity in Landscape gardens - the name reputedly comes from the reaction of onlookers when someone accidentally stumbles into the concealed ditch.

In the 1730s William Kent gradually took over the design and construction of the garden. Kent had begun his career as an artist and spent several successful years in Rome and Florence. He brought his artist's eye and Italian taste to his garden design and later to his architecture when he introduced the Palladian style to England. At Stowe, Kent developed the Landscape appearance of the gardens further, adding rolling fields and more temples and other structures.

In 1741 Lancelot Brown, who became known as Capability Brown, came to Stowe to work as head gardener under Kent. Stowe was where Brown made his name as an 'Improver' of gardens, and from there he went on to an illustrious career developing Landscape Gardens at many estates. Brown continued the softening of the landscape, creating irregular contours to the lake and forming abstract compositions of grass and trees. When Brown left in 1751, he was replaced by the much lesser-known Richard Woodward, who continued Brown's process of naturalization. The family also added more temples and modified existing ones in the neo-classical style using the Italian architect Giovanni Battista Borra.

There were some further modifications later

in the century, and by this point, the garden was already famous, and this was the first garden to have a guide-book written for it. The gardens by that time covered 400 acres, plus a much greater area of surrounding park, which also had temples and gatehouses in it. Often wealthier than the King, the family continued to add more features to the gardens, including at one point a menagerie of rare birds and animals.

However by 1847 the family was in ruins, the property was seized by bailiffs and the Second Duke of Buckingham was forced to flee the country. His son sold most of the contents of the house but made only a small dent in the £1 million family debt. Little was done until 1922 when the house was turned into Stowe School, and some attempt was made to restore the gardens. The house is currently owned by a private trust that has spent £25 million on restoring it. The gardens were passed to the National Trust in 1989 and have been extensively restored since.

The Garden

The gardens at Stowe are the only place where all three of the great developers of the Landscape style,

Bridgeman, Kent and Brown, worked on the same garden. Features developed by each of them can still be seen in the extensive gardens which require multiple visits to be properly appreciated or even seen in their entirety. One-twentieth of all the grade I listed buildings in England can be seen on the grounds of Stowe.

On the south side of the House is the South Vista looking down to the Octagon Lake and further to the Corinthian Arch. The Lake Pavilions are among the earliest buildings designed for the gardens.

To the east of the South Vista is a 40-acre area designed by Kent called the Elysian Fields, a reference to the Greek Elysium, which was a place where dead heroes go, separate from Hades. The area contains buildings dedicated to dead British and Greek heroes, particularly the Temple of British Worthies, containing busts of notable Englishmen as diverse as Shakespeare and King Alfred. Two small lakes are referred to as the River Styx and at the head of one is a Grotto containing a statue of Venus rising from her bath. The melancholy feelings aroused in this area by thoughts of death are enhanced by ivy growing over dead trees that have been deliberately

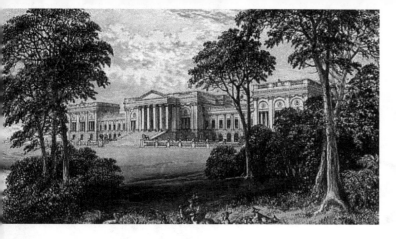

left in place. This is a typical device of the period for encouraging specific feelings in the visitor.

In this area too is the 14th century St Mary's Church, which is all that remains of the old village of Stowe, the Temple of Ancient Virtue and the Cook Monument, commemorating James Cook who died in Hawaii mapping the Pacific Ocean.

Further east is the Hawkwell Field, or Eastern Garden developed during Kent and Brown's period, containing the Gothic Temple, several monuments and the Temple of Friendship. There is also the notable Palladian Bridge over the Octagon Lake and the Queen's Temple. Also in this area are the Saxon Deities, which are copies of an original group of seven statues of the gods who gave their names to the days of the week.

North of Hawkwell Field is the Grecian Valley, which is the first known landscape design entirely by Capability Brown. It contains the Temple of Concord and Victory and a building called the Fane of Pastoral Poetry. Near to the Fane was a group of five shepherds and shepherdesses surrounding a Dancing Faun. These were all sold, but two have been recovered, and there are plans to replace the complete series.

To the west of the South Vista, there is an area containing the Eleven-acre Lake, The Rotondo, and a Temple of Venus designed by William Kent. As well there is a Hermitage, also by Kent, the Artificial Ruins & the Cascade and the Menagerie.

Influences

The gardens at Stowe established the Landscape Garden as the fashion for almost two centuries. It influenced the design of public parks, including Central Park in New York and Hyde Park in London. Across England older gardens were swept away in the rush to 'Improve' country estates and both Kent and Brown became rich – perhaps the

first gardeners to do so. The general face of England, with its scattered woods and rolling fields, was simultaneously the inspiration and the outcome of this movement. It marked an end to geometrical design and the French manner of gardening and the development of a uniquely English landscape.

Further Reading

- Stowe: The Garden and the Park, by Michael Bevington (1996)
- Temples of Delight: Stowe Landscape Gardens, by John Martin Robinson (1994)
- The Genius of the Place: The English Landscape Garden 1620-1820, by John Dixon Hunt and Peter Willis, eds. (1988)
- The Flowering of the Landscape Garden: English Pleasure Grounds 1720-1800, by Mark Laird (1999)
- There are documentaries on Stowe, notably "The Country House" episode of Buildings That Shaped Britain (2006) and "Stowe Gardens" an episode of Abroad Again (2007).

As Seen In...

- Indiana Jones and the Last Crusade (1989)
- Stardust (2007)
- Pan (2015)
- Inspector Morse (1987 TV Series)
- The World Is Not Enough (1999)
- Tomorrow Never Dies (1997)

Practical Information

Stowe is near Buckingham, Buckinghamshire, which is north of London near the town of Milton Keynes.

The gardens are open every day every day of the year except for Christmas Day. Opening hours each day vary with the seasons, and you should consult the National Trust for details: http://www.nationaltrust.org.uk/stowe/opening-times/

HIDCOTE

A Hidden Garden of Eden in Gloucestershire

Hidcote Manor Garden was built in the early 20th century by the Anglo-American Lawrence Johnston. The garden is in The Cotswolds and is famous for its numerous garden 'rooms', enclosed by clipped hedges and containing a wide variety of both common and exotic plants. The design had a strong influence on garden design for the rest of that century.

The Story of Hidcote

We normally assume that gardens are designed by professionals, landscape architects, master gardeners or in earlier times architects and artists. So when seeing the gardens at Hidcote, it can be a shock to discover that this ground-breaking garden was the work of a rank amateur and not even a true Englishman.

Lawrence Waterbury Johnston was born in Paris in 1871, the son of a wealthy Bostonian stock-broker, so he was technically an American, but after graduating from Trinity College at Cambridge University he became a naturalized British subject in 1900 and as if to prove his patriotism, joined the British Army and served in South Africa in the Second Boer War.

Shortly after his military service he joined his now re-married mother, Mrs Gertrude Winthrop, at the house she bought in 1907, Hidcote Manor. This was a 300 acre property in The Cotswolds near the village of Hidcote Bartram, which in turn was near an expat community of American artists at Broadway, Worcestershire. John Singer Sargent was the most prominent of them, and they were joined by British composers and artists such as Edward Elgar, Vaughan Williams, J. M. Barrie and most significantly for Lawrence Johnston's life, the great Arts and Crafts designer William Morris.

Major Johnston, as he was now known, lived a very private life and was shy to the point of being a recluse. An interest in plants had been created by his exposure to the unique flora of South Africa during the Boer War and so he began to design and build gardens around the 17th century Manor house at Hidcote. When they took possession there was no real garden at the Manor, just a large kitchen garden, lawns, and shrubberies.

Johnston created a unique garden at Hidcote. Although the property was large, the actual gardens only occupy 10 acres of it. Because there was no garden before, Johnston took a field and started from scratch, an experience many amateur gardeners can identify with. He did not have the ancient hedges and vistas seen in many older English gardens, and indeed the open, wind-swept nature of his field may have been his inspiration to create not a grand estate but a series of interconnected rooms, many with individual themes and some so small as to rival the smallest town garden today.

We will likely never know the influences on his design since he was too busy gardening to do much writing and too shy to boast of his achievements. We can only see his mind through his work. He was probably inspired by gardening books of the time and one that seems a very likely candidate was The Art and Craft of Garden Making by Thomas H. Mawson, a garden designer of the time. Johnston did not however hire Mawson or for that matter his more famous fellow professional, Edwin Lutyens, but he was influenced by the partnership of Lutyens and the equally famous Gertrude Jekyll. It was Jekyll in particular, with books like Colour in the Flower Garden, published in 1908, that seems to have strongly influenced his innovative development of single colour gardens.

Although he started the gardens shortly after moving into the Manor, the First World War interrupted his gardening, since he was still in the Army. He fought in Flanders and when the war ended returned to his garden. There never were fully-drawn up plans and Johnston probably worked directly on the ground. The gardens at Kiftsgate Court, owned by Heather Muir were very close and the two became friends and exchanged gardening

Lawrence Johnston circa 1927 in Mrs Winthrop's garden with Frank Adams

ideas. Edith Wharton, who also lived nearby and was a lover of Italian gardens, may also have been an influence.

As the garden proceeded he hired a Head Gardener, Frank Adams, and they made an excellent team They visited the Chelsea Flower Show together, as was the style of the time, with owner and gardener consulting over what ideas to incorporate and what plants to buy. During the 1920's he employed 12 full-time gardeners, which was not such a large number as it may at first seem, as large numbers of household and gardening staff was typical of many British homes in this period.

He became especially interested in rare plants and frequently visited the Royal Botanic Gardens in Kew, Surrey. He collected alpine plants which were in vogue at the time and grew hundreds in pots and a rock-garden. He also joined the famed plant collector George Forrest on a plant-collecting expedition to Yunnan, China, and funded expeditions by other collectors.

One of the plants he collected in China, Mahonia siamensis, which was too tender for Hidcote, is still growing in Johnston's second garden, Jardin Serre de la Madone in the hills behind

Menton, France. It was normal at the time for the better-off to winter in the South of France and Menton was a popular destination for the British. Johnston owned this garden from 1924 to his death in 1958 and as the years went on spent more time there and less time at Hidcote. That garden too has been restored and can be visited.

In 1930 Country Life magazine published two articles on the garden and a few years later the famous designer Russell Page made a radio show on it. This increased its fame and the garden began to be open in a limited way to the public – or at least to invited visitors. In 1948 Johnston gave Hidcote to the National Trust and it was the first garden owned by the Trust, who before that had been interested only in houses. For some years the garden was under the control of Graham Thomas, the National Trust's garden consultant, and himself a famous gardener and author. In recent years the plantings have been restored as much as possible to Johnston's original intentions, which were more flamboyant and Edwardian that previously recognized, with more use of tropical plants and annuals for summer display.

The Garden

The Arts and Crafts movement adored the medieval and early Renaissance. In gardens, that meant simple shapes, rectangles, squares, and circles. Part of the genius of Hidcote is the way in which the layout is 'formal,' with simple geometry, but the spaces are filled with a cottage-style profusion of plants. A similar approach can be seen in much of the work of Gertrude Jekyll. In keeping with the Arts and Crafts tradition, all materials used in the garden are natural – various types of stone as paving and low walls, gravel, timber for structures and wrought-iron for gates.

Hedges rather than fences and walls are used to create the enclosures, and Johnston developed the tapestry hedge, using a variety of plants, rather than just one, for some of his hedges. Others are made of the traditional English hedging plant, yew.

The basic layout is a cross, with the shorter axis running from the rear of the Manor House and dominated by a large open lawn area – The Theatre Lawn, 400 feet long surrounded by 7 foot Yew hedges. The cross-axis is formed on one side by the 600 foot long narrow lawn called the Long Walk, which is flanked by deciduous Hornbeam hedges. The axis on the opposite side is not prominent and

is simply a narrow alley flanked by clipped beech trees. This is also the boundary of an area adjoining the house containing work areas and a kitchen garden, as well as the Rose Garden. To either side of the Long Walk is the network of small gardens, each with a different theme and enclosed by various hedges.

Some of the hedges are clipped as topiary, the most prominent being the pair of peacocks in the Fuchsia Garden, which is a square garden with an intricate knot pattern clipped in boxwood. Other themes are the White Garden, the Stilt Garden, with hedges raised on clean trunks and the famous Red Borders, where Johnston created perhaps the first single color garden, a breakthrough comparable to Gainsborough's Blue Boy in art. Other less formal gardens follow the natural stream running across the property and include the woodland areas around the core of the gardens. In all there are over 20 distinct parts to this masterpiece in the articulation of space and the organization of color.

Influence

Hidcote has a great influence in gardens that were to follow it. Most directly related is probably Sissinghurst, the garden created by Vita Sackville-

West in the 1930's. The general concept of order created by lines and hedges, combined with informal planting became the dominant theme of British and to a lesser extend North American garden design for most of the 20th century. The Room Outside, by John Brookes, arguably one of the most influential garden books of the last decades of the 20th century, was inspired by, and promoted, a small-scale version of Johnston's approach.

Johnston had an influence on plants too and one of his plants, a selected form of lavender called Lavandula angustifolia 'Hidcote' is a dwarf English lavender still grown very widely today.

Further Reading

- The Garden at Hidcote, by Fred Whitsey and Tony Lord (2011)
- Hidcote: The Garden and Lawrence Johnston, by Graham S. Pearson (2009)
- Hidcote the Making of a Garden, by E. Clarke (2009)
- Hidcote Manor Garden, by A. Pavord (1993)
- Hidcote Manor Garden: Hidcote Bartrim, by V. Sackville-West (1952)
- There is a television documentary – Hidcote: A Garden for all Seasons (2011) featuring

the work of the current head gardener, Glyn Jones, to uncover more about the very private Major Johnston and his garden.

As Seen In...

- Miss Marple: Nemesis (1987)
- Britain's Finest (2003)

Practical Information

The address of the Manor is Hidcote Bartrim, near Chipping Campden, Gloucestershire. The garden is close to Stratford-on-Avon and could be fitted in with a visit there.

The gardens are open every day from May to the end of September. They are only open on Saturday and Sunday from November to the end of February. In March, April and October they are open on some weekdays as well as weekends and you should consult the National Trust for precise days in those periods and for actual opening hours each day, which vary with the seasons. http://www.nationaltrust.org.uk/hidcote/opening-times/

HESTERCOMBE

An Iconic Lutyens Lanscape in Somerset

Hestercombe is a garden in Somerset which features both a 17th century Landscape Garden and an important Edwardian garden by the design team of Edward Lutyens and Gertrude Jekyll. The garden is a high-point of their partnership and marks the beginning of the 20th century English garden style.

The Story

The estate at Hestercombe dates back to Anglo-Saxon times and was occupied by the Warres family from 1391 until 1872. In the second half of the 18th century, the grounds were laid out in the Landscape Style by Coplestone Warre Bampfylde, a talented classicist, and a friend and advisor to Henry Hoare at the nearby estate of Stourhead. The gardens he created can still be seen beside the later garden and Hestercombe is perhaps a unique opportunity to see two major design styles of English gardens at a single site.

In 1872, Miss Elizabeth Warre, who was the last member of the Warre family, died and the property was purchased by the 1st Viscount Portman, who carried out extensive re-modelling of the house. His grandson, the Hon Edward Portman, commissioned Edwin Lutyens to create a new formal garden in 1903.

The architect Edward Lutyens had not yet begun his work for the War Graves Commission following WWI, or his creation of the new capital of British India, the city of Delhi, in the 1920s, for which he was to be knighted, but he did already have a reputation for his homes, which were in the Arts and Crafts tradition and featured superb craftsmanship and handwork. He had also met the garden designer Gertrude Jekyll when in 1896 he designed her home at Munstead Wood, in Surrey. They had gone on to develop a partnership as garden designers.

Lutyens and Jekyll had developed a style that combined a formal classicism and a use of natural materials such as brick and stone, with an informal approach to planting, using hardy shrubs and perennial plants in arrangements that aimed to display little apparent order, but which in fact blended colours and forms with a new subtleness that would set the style for the next century. Lutyens did most of the layout of the beds, paths and walls and Jekyll chose and organized the plantings.

Gertrude Jekyll (pronounced with a double-e like 'Jeep') was born in 1843, and she was one of those rare individuals who combine an artistic talent with a love for and understanding of science. She studied art at the South Kensington School of Art in London, but also studied botany, optics and the science of colour. She was greatly attracted to the work of the French chemist Michel Eugène Chevreul, whose technical book, The Principles of Harmony and Contrast of Colours, published in 1854, was the first work to address the effect of colours on each other and the creation of harmony between colours. She knew William Morris and like Lutyens had been absorbed into Romanticism and the Arts and Crafts Movement.

In gardening she was strongly influenced by William Robinson, who had broken with the 19th century use of tender 'bedding plants', such as geraniums and petunias, in formal, rigid designs that used primary colours and simple colour contrasts. Robinson had an influential gardening magazine (which Jekyll was to write extensively for) that championed the use of hardy perennial flowers, bulbs, and flowering shrubs to bring colour without the artificiality of Victorian bedding schemes.

After Lutyens designed Munstead Wood for her mother, Gertrude designed the garden around their home and this soon made her well-known, leading to commissions for garden designs and her partnership with Lutyens. Hestercombe is often considered the high-point of that partnership and it is also the most accessible of their gardens.

In 1944 the property was taken by the Crown Estates in lieu of death duties and had various used during the rest of last century. The house and gardens are now managed by a charitable trust, and in recent years the gardens have been restored to the original Lutyens/Jekyll plans.

The Gardens

The gardens are in two distinct parts, connected on a grand scale by stone steps descending a grassy, terraced bank, known as the Daisy Steps, designed by Lutyens.

The 16 acres of Landscape Garden designed by C.W. Bampfylde were largely lost during the 19th century but have been restored. Although not comparable with other great designs of the 18th century it does give a good picture of the Picturesque style of that time. There are two ponds,

the lower one called the Pear Pond, connected by a cascade which flows into a stream with a series of small cascades running through the Valley of Cascades, designed in 1791. Further down is the Great Cascade down a rocky bank, which can be viewed from an adjacent grassy terrace. There are numerous vantage points offering views beyond the garden across the Taunton valley. There are excellent views from the Gothic Alcove, the excavation of a Bampfylde summer house from 1761. Other features include a Friendship Urn dedicated to his friendship with Henry Hoare, the restored Temple Arbour and a Witch House.

It is the Lutyens/Jekyll garden however which is the main attraction at Hestercombe, and this is situated behind the house. The garden begins directly behind the south side of the house, where a rectangular grass terrace built during the late 19th century has been retained. To the west of the upper terrace there is a large Rose Garden, featuring old and rare varieties of roses. To the east, there is an entrance into an enclosed area which is the pivot of the garden. This area – The Rotunda – is enclosed by circular walls and features a central pond with detailed and complex patterns in stone paving

radiating from it.

The exit from the Rotunda to the east leads into a long garden dominated by an Orangery. This is a single-storey structure with tall arched windows, designed in the style of Christopher Wren. These buildings were features of gardens in earlier centuries as places to grow tender plants, especially citrus trees and pre-date the technology needed to build full greenhouses. Beyond the garden containing the Orangery is an entrance into The Dutch Garden, which is not really a Dutch Garden at all. Typical Dutch Gardens in the English garden context feature elaborate topiary, but although this garden has a formal plan, with stone paving, it features perennial plants such as lavender, catmint, roses, hardy fuchsias and a Jekyll favourite, the hardy Yucca filamentosa with its tall spikes of large, fragrant white flowers.

On the south side of the terrace behind the house, the garden descends in narrow terraces to the main feature, The Great Plat, a large formal square garden which carries undertones of Victorian bedding schemes but is an attempt to create a new style of formalism. This area is a little over 100 feet square, with a large cross of lawn on the diagonal

and smaller beds between the arms of the cross. The design is edged in paving stones, and the planting is not tender plants but groups of perennial plants and small shrubs. The Plat is sunken below the surrounding area so that it can be looked down on from the sides, in the manner of many Renaissance formal gardens. There are semi-circular stone steps in the four corners linking the upper and lower levels.

On either side are two identical gardens, The Water Gardens, which feature a narrow central water canal in brick, linking three round pools constructed with different depths to accommodate different species of water plants. The sides of these levels are planted with perennial beds.

The water in the canals flows over the edge into tanks placed on a slightly lower level that encloses the Great Plat to the south. Here there is a long walk featuring a 200 foot pergola with views overlooking the valley. The Pergola is covered with climbing roses and other climbing plants.

The whole garden is a series of levels, looking onto each other, or creating privacy, connected by steps and entered through arches. Terraces are often edged in stone balustrades. There are numerous urns, walls decorated with cherubs and other ornamentation displaying skilled craftsmanship. These changes in levels and the views and vistas created are an integral part of the design and feel of this garden.

Influence

Lutyens & Jekyll gardens are characterised by their combination of formality in layout, the use of natural materials in the Arts and Crafts tradition and complex informal plantings featuring subtle colour combinations and shifts. Hestercombe displays this perhaps better than any of their gardens still in existence.

The garden is a pivotal change from Victorian bedding schemes with their intrinsic artificiality and the Landscape Garden, which emphasised semi-natural landscape at the expense of variety in plant material. The Hestercombe garden style has been called the Architectural Garden, which combines strong structure with natural planting in a way that was to dominate the 20th century garden design. It also allowed gardeners the opportunity to use the vast array of exotic plants, both wild and the products of plant breeding, that had become available towards the end of the 19th century and later, but had not found a real place in gardens before.

Further Reading

There is no single book on Hestercombe, but the garden is featured in numerous books on English gardens and on the life of Gertrude Jekyll. Some good starting points would be:

- The Story of Gardening, by Penelope Hobhouse (2002)
- The Oxford Companion to Gardens, by Patrick Goode, Michael Lancaster, Geoffrey Jellicoe & Susan Jellicoe (2001)
- The Gardens of Gertrude Jekyll, by Richard Bisgrove (1992)
- Gardens of a Golden Afternoon: The Story of a Partnership, Edwin Lutyens & Gertrude Jekyll, by Jane Brown (1982)

Most of Gertrude Jekyll's books on gardening can still be found in various editions and reprints. Some titles are:

- Wood and Garden (1899)
- Home and garden (1900)
- Roses for English Gardens (1902)
- Colour in the flower garden (1908)
- Children and gardens (1908)
- Colour schemes for the flower garden (1919)

Practical Information

Hestercombe is managed as a private charity. It is situated in the village of Cheddon Fitzpaine, north of the town of Taunton, Somerset.

The gardens are open every day of the year, including all holidays, except for December 25th. The gardens are open from 10:00 am to 6:00 pm in summer and from 10:00 am to 5:00 pm in winter. Further information can be obtained from the garden's website: http://www.hestercombe.com/

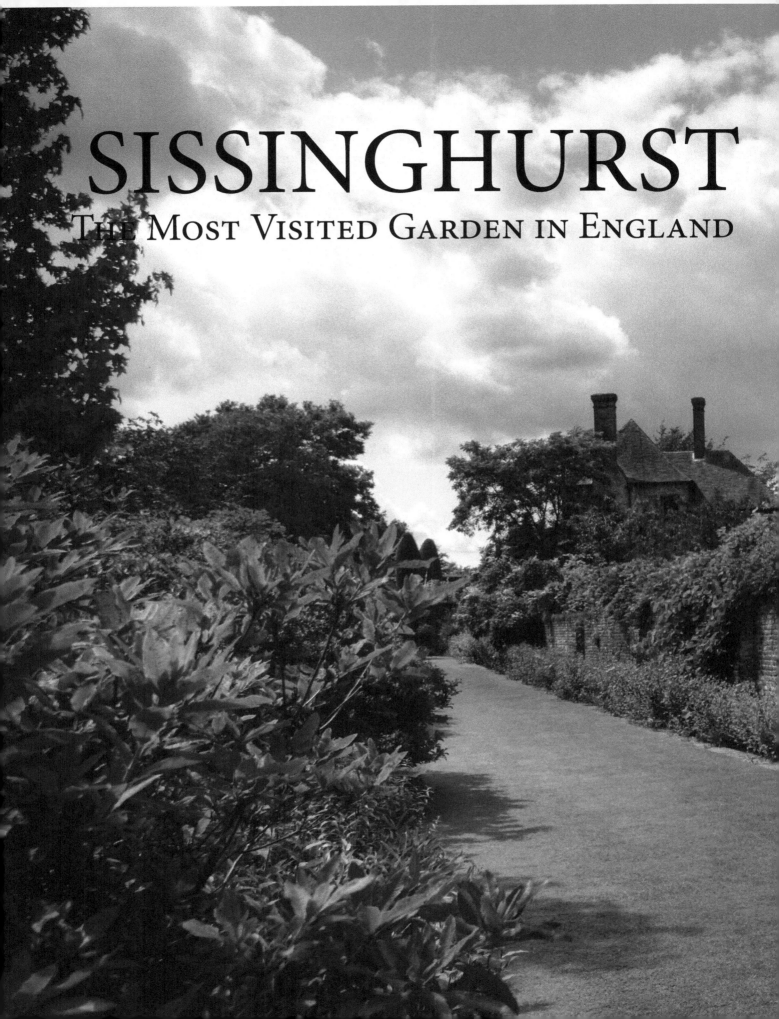

SISSINGHURST

The Most Visited Garden in England

Sissinghurst is a garden in Kent and is the most visited garden in England. It was created in the 1930's by Vita Sackville-West and her husband, Harold Nicholson. The garden features a series of rooms each with a distinct theme and separated by yew hedges and ancient walls. The garden had a profound influence on the development of English gardens.

The Story Behind Sissinghurst

When The Honourable Victoria Mary Sackville-West, usually known as Vita, was born, it would have been known immediately that as a female she would not inherit her family home, Knole House, in Kent. The property passed to her father's cousin, an event that would haunt Vita for her whole life. So in 1930 when she and her husband Sir Harold George Nicolson, found a ruined Elizabethan tower at a derelict farm in the village of Sissinghurst, Kent, she saw the opportunity to replace Knole House with her own historic estate. Queen Elizabeth I had spent three nights at Sissinghurst Castle, which had belonged to a Privy Councillor of Henry VIII, so its credentials were propitious.

Vita and Harold had married when Vita was 21, in 1913. Even by modern standards, they had an 'interesting' marriage. Both were homosexual, and both had numerous liaisons with other people, yet they were close and devoted to each other. Perhaps Vita's most famous partner was Virginia Woolf, who used Vita as a model for the main male character Orlando in her eponymously named novel. They had two sons, Benedict and Nigel. Vita was part of the Bloomsbury Group, a progressive collection of artists and writers who mostly lived in that part of London, near the British Museum.

When they bought the 450 acres with the Castle, farmhouse and surrounding fields they enjoyed a certain genteel poverty and the money to maintain their lifestyle and implement their plans was always in short supply. So the garden developed over a long period and two years of work was needed even before it could be lived in. However by 1938 Vita and Harold were opening the garden to the public for sixpence a visit.

Vita passed away in 1962 and Harold in 1968. To avoid paying estate duties their son, Nigel handed the property over to the National Trust. Vita would not have been happy – when she had been forced to sign over her interests in Knole House in 1947 to the National Trust she said it was "a betrayal of all the tradition of my ancestors and the house I loved."

Part of the agreement with the National Trust was that the heirs could continue to live in the property. The current resident is their grandson, Adam Nicolson, who with his wife Sarah Raven is attempting to gain greater control over the direction of the garden and farm. There had always been a tradition of having a female, lesbian, head gardener at Sissinghurst, but following disputes with the incumbent Alexis Datta, this tradition was broken with the hiring of Troy Scott-Smith for the post. This new head gardener is more in tune with the plans of Adam and Sarah and has also spoken of replacing some of the traditional plantings with plants "more of Vita's artistic spirit" but implicitly not actually used by her, perhaps because they did not exist or were unavailable during her years. This would be in direct opposition to the emphasis in the National Trust on authenticity in restoration.

The Garden

Sissinghurst Garden occupies just 5 acres, but it is the most visited garden in England and probably the most influential. Vita and Harold were inspired by the ideas and gardens created at the beginning of the 20th century by Gertrude Jekyll and Edwin Lutyens and by Hidcote Manor, begun some 20 years earlier by the Anglo-American Lawrence Johnston. They did a good part of the physical work themselves as well as employing gardeners. Their goal was to create a series of rooms opening into each other and with inviting vistas between them. In all, there are ten distinct sections to the garden. Harold was responsible for laying out the 'rooms' and Vita chose the plants. The rooms are created by a combination of old walls from the original buildings and yew hedges. Each garden has a specific theme and combines the simplicity and austerity of squares and circles created by the hedges and wall with an exuberance of plant material chosen with great taste by Vita.

The entrance areas in the Upper and Lower Courtyards are large formal lawns flanked by borders of perennials flowers, including a Purple Border. These areas are greatly enhanced, as are other sections of the garden, by the ancient red-brick walls remaining from the original buildings of the Castle.

Perhaps the most famous area is the White Garden, which contains beds edged with boxwood in a simple geometrical pattern. The planting is of course entirely with white flowers and has been a continuous inspiration to home gardeners. White gardens are easy to plant, there is no shortage of white flowers to choose from, but they are more successful in the cloudy climate of England than when reproduced in sunnier places, where the white loses its interest in the glare of sunlight.

The Rose Garden is larger and is built in quarters around a lawn enclosed by circular yew hedges. Vita was one of the first people to collect and appreciate the so-called 'old roses,' varieties from previous centuries dating back to the Middle Ages. These often have exquisite forms and scents but normally only flower once a year and had been displaced in the 19th century by the development of roses that bloom more or less continuously. This garden is at its peak therefore in June when the roses bloom, so to extend the season of interest later-flowering perennials and Clematis vines are also grown.

The property had a small brick cottage on it, used by Harold as a workroom. Here they built the Cottage Garden, in imitation of the casual style as-sociated with the humble gardens of English country-folk. Edwin Lutyens designed a bench for this area which has been widely copied.

From the Rose Garden and the Cottage Garden, one enters the Lime Walk, which is a narrow, rectangular garden of spring bulbs with a double row of Lime trees clipped to a hedge but elevated on their trunks in a manner called 'pleaching.' This area reflects Harold's interest in classical Italian gardens and ends with niches cut into the hedges containing statues. There are large Tuscan terracotta pots along the walk which are planted with flowers for the summer, and they are the only colour in this area once the spring bulbs have finished blooming.

The Lime Walk, in turn, enters a more informal area called The Nuttery which as might be expected is an orchard of Hazelnut trees under-planted with spring bulbs, primroses, ferns and other spring-flowering plants.

At the end of The Nuttery, there is an Herb Garden with over 100 types of herbs, laid out in a simple plan of symmetrically arranged beds. The layout is very much in the manner of medieval herb gardens found in Monasteries. This was one of the first parts of the garden designed and planted and shows Vita's passion for old plants and the extent of her knowledge of them.

Beside the Nuttery and Herb Garden is The Orchard, filled with apple trees with roses climbing into them and planted underneath with thousands of daffodils. This area is left under long grass for the summer although several walks are mowed into it to allow access. Two sides of the Orchard are flanked by the only remaining sections of the original moat which surrounded the castle.

The old Elizabethan double Tower which captured the hearts of Vita and Harold was eventually restored, and from the top, there is an excellent view of the garden laid out below and of the surrounding estate and countryside.

The genius of Sissinghurst and its essence is the interplay between the formal elements developed by Harold from his love of Italian and other formal gardens countered and balanced by the extraordinary exuberance of Vita's planting, where roses climb into hedges and trees, thyme spills out and invaded the lawns and Jackson Pollack outbursts of colour are restrained by the dense, dark frames of yew and boxwood. This melding of the medieval with the wild had been pioneered at Hidcote Manor by Lawrence Johnston, but at Sissinghurst the wildness and the restraint are always poised to overwhelm each other, creating an exciting tension and perhaps a metaphor for their marriage.

Influence

Sissinghurst, with its various elements and themes, was extraordinarily influential in the shape of British gardens for much of the 20th century. White Gardens sprang up in every suburb and daffodils planted in grass became a gorgeous cliché. Collections of old roses and colourful perennial borders were de rigueur for all serious gardens. Only towards the end of the century did modernism become more acceptable and with the growth of ecological gardening collections of exotic and rare plants and varieties are being replaced by the cultivation of native and 'natural' plants.

Further Reading

- Gardening at Sissinghurst, by Tony Lord (2000)
- Planting Schemes from Sissinghurst by Tony Lord (2000)
- Sissinghurst Castle — An illustrated history, by Nigel Nicolson, (1964)
- Sissinghurst — The Making of a Garden, by Anne Scott-James (1974)
- Sissinghurst: Vita Sackville-West and the Creation of a Garden, by Vita Sackville-West and Sarah Raven (2014)
- Vita's Other World: A Gardening Biography of V. Sackville-West, by Jane Brown, (1985)
- Vita's grand-son has written a book on his dealings with the National Trust and his attempt to revitalize the surrounding farmlands as an organic farm. This is described in his book Sissinghurst: An Unfinished History, by Adam Nicolson (2008). There is also an 8-part television documentary series called Sissinghurst (2009) about the garden and Adam Nicolson's plans for the farm.

As Seen In...

- Portrait of a Marriage (1990 Mini-Series)
- Around the World in 80 Gardens (2008 TV Series)
- Britain's Finest (2003 TV Series)
- Sissinghurst (2009 TV Series)

Practical Information

The address of the Castle and Garden is Biddenden Road, near Cranbrook, Kent. It is two miles north-east of Cranbrook, which is east of Tunbridge Wells.

The gardens are open every day of the year, including all holidays. The restaurant and shop have more restricted openings, and guided tours are not always available. You should consult the National Trust for opening hours each day, which vary with the seasons. http://www.nationaltrust.org.uk/sissinghurst-castle/opening-times/

10 INTERESTING FACTS ABOUT CAPABILITY BROWN

By John Rabon

One of the world's most prolific landscape architects, Lancelot "Capability" Brown left his mark on Britain in the 18th Century. During his career, Brown touched the landscapes of many locations in a way that is still visible today. Whether he was working for royalty, aristocracy, clergy, or the public, his reputation was one for working in harmony with nature, bringing out the innate beauty of the surroundings. Baptised 30 August 1716 in Northumberland, Brown would rise from humble beginnings to become King George III's Master Gardener. Though his influence waned as the Romantic movement took hold in the 19th Century, much of his influence remains.

Fast Work

Brown had a reputation for working quickly. When surveying a property before transforming it, Capability Brown used his expert equestrian skills to complete his preliminary work at a fast pace, often taking no more than an hour to survey a huge.

Training

Capability Brown was born the son of a yeoman farmer and a chambermaid, and at sixteen, he attended Cambo School before apprenticing as a gardener's boy under the head gardener for Sir William Lorraine. He then moved onto Sir Richard Granville's Estate, Wotton, and then to the gardening staff of Lord Cobham at Stowe. It was during his time at Stowe that he began to develop a reputation with the landed gentry, often showing them around the grounds. This permitted him to start working as an independent designer and contractor, beginning the career for which he would become famous.

Moving Up Fast

Brown became the Master Gardener of Stowe when he was only twenty-six years old.

What's in a Nickname?

Brown's nickname "Capability" came from a particular catchphrase. He we would often tell his clients that their properties had "great capabilities."

He's Got Style

While at Stowe, Brown worked under William Kent, one of the earliest pioneers of the English Style of gardening.

This style relied heavily on making the landscape look simultaneously elegant and natural. Brown would often employ a sunk fence or a "ha-ha" ditch to make separate parts of the garden appear to be one continuous piece. Despite his bringing out the already existing natural beauty of a place, he was often criticised for his habit of wiping away the works of previous gardeners to create his own unique vision.

Decidedly Not French

In many ways, Brown's style was a contrast to that of French landscape architect Andre Le Notre, who preferred to impose his will upon a landscape, often clearing land and reshaping it to fit his designs. One of the best examples of his work are the palace gardens of Versailles. Brown preferred an approach that was more in tune with the pre-existing landscape.

That's a Lot of Gardens

Brown was responsible for creating over 170 gardens during his career. Amongst the works you can see today are: Highclere Castle, Blenheim Palace, Milton Abbey, and Hampton Court Palace, amongst others. During the 18th Century, is was more uncommon for him to have *not* designed the gardens of an estate than to have added his considerable influence.

A Menu of Options

Brown had several services that he was willing to provide for his clients. He could provide a survey and then leave it to the client to have someone else carry out the work. Other times he would provide a foreman to carry out the work with labour provided by the estate. Lastly, he would oversee all the work himself. When Brown opened an account with Drummond's Bank in 1753, he had only four foremen, but by the end the decade, he employed nearly twenty.

Heavenly Works

Such was Brown's wide influence on British landscapes that English poet and satirist Richard Owen Cambridge joked that he hoped to die before Brown so that he could "see heaven before it was improved."

The Sheriff is Near!

In 1770, Capability Brown was made the High Sheriff of Huntingdonshire.

THE ROYAL BOTANIC GARDENS

ONE OF THE MOST IMPORTANT BOTANIC GARDENS IN THE WORLD

Many visitors to England stay in London and may not have the time to visit gardens outside the city. However, with a short Tube ride, it is possible to visit one of the most important gardens in the world. The Royal Botanic Gardens Kew, has been a center of botanical and gardening activity for over 250 years and is still the preeminent center for plant knowledge. The gardens contain the world's largest collection of plants in one place, growing in greenhouses from the 19th , 20th and 21st centuries, formal and informal outdoor gardens and innovative plantings of all kinds.

The Story

The area to the southwest of London known as Kew has had permanent Royal associations since 1501, when Henry V built Sheen Palace, later to become Richmond Palace, nearby. In 1522, Mary Tudor built a house in Kew, with a drive connecting it to Richmond Palace. In 1600, the area that would become Kew Gardens was described as a farm field.

The early beginnings of a garden for exotic plants on the site at Kew Park, built by Lord Capel John of Tewkesbury, was enlarged and developed in the 18th century by the Dowager Princess of Wales, Princess Augusta. She employed Sir William Chambers, an architect and designer in the fashionable Chinoiserie style to construct several buildings in the gardens, including the Pagoda, built in 1761 and still standing.

The Orangery, designed by Chambers, was also erected in 1761. This was an early attempt to overwinter citrus trees, which were then put outdoors during the summer. However, the technology of the time did not allow for large enough windows. This lack of light, combined with fumes from early heating systems, made growing the plants very difficult. The building is now a restaurant.

George III enjoyed the gardens, purchasing the building now known as Kew Palace as a nursery for his children. He also sought the assistance of Sir Joseph Banks in developing the site. The botanist Banks had just returned from traveling with Captain Cook on his voyage to Australia, and he arranged for more plants to be collected from around the world. The plants from these collections formed the basis for the Royal Botanic Gardens collections which would make them the most important botanical

gardens in the world.

The first garden was under the directorship of William Aiton, who was appointed in 1759 and continued until his death in 1793. He published Hortus Kewensis, the first list of plants growing in the gardens, and still an invaluable resource for knowledge on the introduction of plants into England.

William Aiton was succeeded by his son, William Townsend Aiton, as director of the gardens. W.T. Aiton was also an important founding member of The Royal Horticultural Society (famous for the Chelsea Show held every May) and together with William Cavendish, director of the RHS, worked to establish Kew as the national botanic gardens. Cavendish grew a banana in the greenhouses at Kew which became the Cavendish variety, still the major commercial banana around the world today. The gardens were also instrumental in establishing rubber plantations in British colonies outside the tree's native South America.

W.T. Aiton was succeeded in 1841 as director at Kew by the already famous botanist William Hooker. Hooker was an assiduous worker for botany and he had a botanist attached to every

British expedition at a time when the Royal Navy was sailing the world and mapping it accurately for the first time. He also expanded the gardens from 10 acres to 75, plus an additional 270 acres of tree collections, the approximate area of the present-day gardens. Like Aiton, he was succeeded as director by his son, Sir Joseph Dalton Hooker.

In the 20th century, the gardens continued the work of collecting and studying plants, moving more strongly to a conservation-orientated approach, with a seed-bank and numerous conservation projects.

Originally funded by the Department of Agriculture, towards the end of the last century the gardens was made an independent public body under a board of trustees, partly funded by government and partly by its own efforts. This has led to a more populist approach, with public concerts and events held regularly in the gardens and a greater emphasis on marketing the image of the gardens and broadening its appeal to general visitors.

The Gardens

The heart of Kew is its plant collections. There

are 30,000 different plants growing in the various sections of the gardens, and the pressed plant collection of over seven million specimens is one of the largest in the world. About 250 scientists work in various areas of research, and the gardens provide a range of training courses for practical gardening.

Approximately half the area of the gardens is taken up by the Arboretum, a collection of over 14,000 different varieties of trees drawn from all over the world. An aerial view of parts of this collection can be seen from the Treetop Walkway, 60 feet up and almost 700 feet long. Access is by steps or elevator. Plant collections in the Arboretum include Rhododendrons and Azaleas, Magnolias, Lilacs and Bamboos.

Flowering plants are organized botanically in the Herbaceous Grounds, to show their relationships. They are also gathered together in various collections, including the Aquatic Garden, Grass Garden, Rock Garden and Rose Garden. Annual flowers are used extensively throughout the grounds, particularly in a formal display in front of the Palm House.

The various greenhouses contain collections of plants too tender to be grown outdoors. The most well-known is the Palm House. This iconic structure was built by Decimus Burton in the 1840s and was the first large-scale use of wrought-iron in construction. Each of the curved panes of glass was, and still is, handmade. The house contains palms and other tropical plants and is 60 feet high in the tallest section to accommodate large trees.

The Temperate House, which is the largest Victorian greenhouse still in existence, covering 53,000 square feet, was built a few decades later. It contains trees, shrubs and plants arranged by geographic origin, from Australia, South Africa, and South America.

In 1987, the slightly smaller Princess of Wales Conservatory, designed by Gordon Wilson, replaced earlier orchid houses. This greenhouse complex has ten climate zones, controlled by computers, allowing plants from many different habitats to be grown successfully. It displays the Orchid Collection, the Cacti Collection, Bromeliad Collection and the Carnivorous Plants Collection, and includes a pond displaying the world's largest water lily, Victoria amazonica, which can be viewed from both above and below water.

Delicate mountain plants are displayed in the Alpine House, an arching structure opened in 2006.

As well as the Pagoda, the gardens also contain the Chokushi-Mon, a replica of a Japanese gateway, built in 1910 and a Japanese Minka House, added in 2001. There are also two Galleries dedicated to botanical art.

Further Reading

- The Gardens at Kew, by Allen Paterson and Andrew McRobb
- In for a Penny: A Prospect of Kew Gardens, by Wilfrid Blunt (the reference is to the original entry fee)
- The History of the Royal Botanic Gardens Kew, by Ray Desmond
- The Story of Kew Gardens in Photographs, by Lynn Parker and Kiri Ross-Jones
- Kew: Gardens for Science and Pleasure, by Kew Royal Botanic Gardens

As Seen In...

- Rosemary & Thyme (2003 TV Series)
- Carry on Up the Jungle (1970)
- Time Team Episode: Kew Gardens, London (2003)

Practical Information

The address of the Garden is Kew, Richmond, Surrey. Kew Gardens Tube Station is 400 yards from Victoria Gate, one of the four entrances to the gardens.

Road trains tour the large area of the gardens, and guided tours are also available.

The gardens are open from 10 am every day. Closing times vary with the seasons between 4:15 pm in winter to 7:30 pm on weekends in summer. Greenhouses close 30 minutes earlier, but never later than 5:30 pm. The two art galleries are closed on Mondays.

GREAT DIXTER

A Quintessential English Style Garden

Great Dixter, in Sussex, was the home of the garden writer Christopher Lloyd, who promoted a particularly 'English' style of gardening, based on the Arts & Crafts movement of the 19th and early 20th century. The medieval house was remodelled for Lloyd's father by Edward Lutyens, and today it is run by a trust, preserving Lloyd's approach and style to gardening. Both the garden and house can be visited.

The Story of Great Dixter

On the southeast coast of England lies Hastings, site of the famous battle of 1066, known to every British schoolchild and most visitors, too. A few miles to the north of Hastings is the small village of Northiam. This part of England is the Sussex Weald, a medieval forested area now a patchwork of forest and fields, across rolling hills studded with outcrops of sandstone.

Just outside Northiam, there was a manor house, called Dicksterve, dating back to 1220. In the 15th century, the house had been rebuilt and had become the property of the 1st Duke of Windsor. Over the centuries it passed through various hands and in 1910, after being on the market for ten years, it was purchased by Nathanial Lloyd. Lloyd was approaching 60 and had been born into a wealthy middle-class family. He had made his own fortune with a color printing business making the then ubiquitous posters for advertising, which are so collectible today. A few years earlier Lloyd had married the much younger Daisy Field, a solicitor's daughter and descendant of Oliver Cromwell. He purchased the manor, now known as Dixter, for his retirement, to enjoy shooting and golf.

Lloyd was a man of taste, and he hired the architect Edwin Lutyens, who already had a reputation for country houses in the Arts & Crafts tradition, to expand and develop the house. For £75 he purchased a derelict yeoman's cottage, built in the 16th century, and transported it from Benenden in nearby Kent, to Dixter. Lutyens used this cottage to create the master bedroom and other rooms, adding sections in the same medieval style, preserving most of the features of the original homes and linking them into a unified whole. Now much larger than its original, it was re-named Great Dixter. The house was completed by 1912, and in 1913 it was featured in Country Life magazine.

Lutyens was also known for his gardens, and with Nathanial, they designed the original gardens around the house. In 1921, Daisy gave birth to a son, Christopher, the first in a family that eventually grew to six children. The young Christopher soon took an active interest in the gardens, helping his mother do the actual work to actualize his father's designs and ideas. Daisy introduced Christopher to Gertrude Jekyll, the gardening associate of Lutyens, a famous gardener, and designer in her own right.

After Rugby School, Cambridge University and service in the Second World War, Christopher went to Wye College in nearby Kent, an agricultural college and a branch of the University of London. He graduated in 1949 with a degree in Decorative Horticulture, specializing in garden design and management. For a time, he stayed at Wye College as an assistant lecturer, but in 1954 he returned to Great Dixter. His father had died in 1933 and Daisy, often described as 'formidable,' was running the household. Christopher created a small nursery specializing in the rare plants grown in the gardens and often opened the house and grounds to the public. Lloyd's first book, The Mixed Border, was published in 1957, promoting the then novel idea of growing shrubs and herbaceous plants together in the same beds. In 1963, he started a regular gardening column in Country Life, which continued until just before his death, which provided a vehicle for him to promote his ideas and enthusiasms and made him widely known. He was also the gardening correspondent for the Guardian newspaper.

Further books followed, and he became known as what the English call a 'plants man' – someone with great knowledge of plants, their taxonomy, botany, cultivation and aesthetic character. He had a reputation for being both helpful and spontaneous, once inviting a group of Hungarian students to stay in the house after his dachshunds ate their sandwiches. However, he did not, as the saying goes, suffer fools gladly, sometimes refusing to name a plant for a visitor if they lacked seriousness and a notebook ready to write the name down in.

Daisy Lloyd died in 1977 and Christopher inherited the property, continuing to expand and develop the gardens, later with his protégé and head gardener Fergus Garrett setting the pace and encouraging novelty and experimentation. He traveled extensively, giving lecture tours in the USA and elsewhere, promoting the use of rarer plants

and a high-maintenance, Arts & Crafts style of gardening on a grand scale, as well as encouraging the use of unusual trees and shrubs in ordinary gardens. He was regularly seen in his gardens as an anonymous worker in the beds, weeding and trimming.

Christopher Lloyd died following a stroke on January the 27th, 2006, a few weeks before his 85th birthday. He had established a charitable trust to continue the life of Great Dixter, and that trust is currently responsible for the gardens.

The Gardens

The gardens at Great Dixter are still under the control of Fergus Garrett and his team of five to six gardeners. Garrett continues to work within Lloyd's framework of unusual plants grown in novel combinations and with constant experimentation – a sophisticated form of play raised to the level of high art. Unusual and even outrageous colour schemes are used, and a mixture of formal and informal elements runs throughout the garden.

The gardens surround the house on all sides, still largely following the original compartmental layout designed by Edward Lutyens. Yew hedges create the compartments, and additional yew topiary is scattered around the grounds. There are few neat lawns, most of the grassy areas are filled with flowering plants and grown as meadows with infrequent mowing. Brick arches connect the sections of the garden, and the paths are made with York stone, originally used for London sidewalks and widely sold for garden use when the stone was replaced by asphalt.

To the south of the house lies The Orchard, with a variety of fruit trees and spring bulbs growing in the grass, which is mowed once a year, in summer.

To the east are a series of semi-formal gardens containing the major plant collections and the famous Long Border – 210 feet long and 15 feet deep, planted with a mixture of shrubs and flowers, the inspiration for Lloyd's first book. The Peacock Garden, with 18 topiary birds and the High Garden

are other main features in this area.

To the north of the house are more informal plantings, with annual flowers and meadow gardens. There is also the Sunk Garden, designed by Lloyd's father, with a central pond. An old rose garden designed by Lutyens is now the Exotic Garden, featuring a wild display of tropical and sub-tropical plants planted out each summer.

Besides flowers, Lloyd had a keen interest in growing vegetables and cooking them. The Vegetable Garden continues to be cultivated at the far eastern end of the gardens.

Further Reading

- Christopher Lloyd's writing includes:
- The Mixed Border (1957)
- Clematis (1965)
- The Well-Tempered Garden (1970)
- In My Garden: The Garden Diaries of Great Dixter (1993 – a collection of his Country Life columns)

- Exotic Planting for Adventurous Gardeners (2007) [completed after his death by colleagues]

Practical Information

The address of the Garden is Great Dixter, Dixter Road, Northiam, Rye, East Sussex.

The gardens are open from late March to late October, from Tuesday to Sunday and on Holiday Mondays. Entrance is between 11 am and 5 pm (last admission) for the gardens, and from 2 pm to 5 pm for the house.

BODNANT GARDEN

FOUR GENERATIONS OF WELSH GARDENING

Bodnant Garden is in the north of Wales, near Snowdonia National Park. It was begun around 1875 and has been in the same family for four generations. It is famous for its formal flower gardens but more so for its Rhododendrons and Azaleas and its extensive botanical collections of rare and unusual plants from around the world collected by botanists on expeditions sponsored by the family.

The Story

Henry Davis Pochin was a successful industrial chemist who, in the 19th century, developed new processes for manufacturing soap and for paper-making. In 1874, wealthy from his inventions, a coal-mine director and a member of Parliament, Pochin bought the Bodnant estate in the Conwy valley in northern Wales. The estate consisted of 25 tenant farms, a house and 80 acres of garden. He lived there in 'active retirement' until his death in 1895. A branch of the Hiraethlyn River, which itself empties into the Conwy River, runs through an area of the garden known as The Dell, and there Pochin set about planting a wide variety of conifers from the Americas and the Far East.

Henry Davis Pochin had a daughter, Laura, who in 1877 married Charles Benjamin Bright McLaren. He was a barrister, but soon followed family tradition into politics and became an MP, eventually joining the Privy Council. In 1910 he left the Commons and his son took his seat in Parliament. The following year he was rewarded for his services by being raised to the Peerage as Baron Aberconway. When Pochin died McLaren inherited his industrial holdings, which he developed, chairing several important companies, including the Scottish shipbuilders John Brown & Company, English China Clays and the Metropolitan Railway Company. The latter was responsible for the early stages of the London Underground, including the Metropolitan and Circle Lines.

His son Henry also began his career as a barrister, but entered politics in 1906 and became Private Under-Secretary to David Lloyd George, who at the time was President of the Board of Trade. From 1910 to 1922 he held his father's seat in the Commons. He showed an interest in aesthetics and in 1915 he founded the Design and Industries Association, a group established to develop and

improve British industrial design in reaction to the more advanced developments taking place in Germany. His aesthetic interests also extended to plants and gardening and long before inheriting the estate on his father's death in 1934 he was developing the gardens at Bodnant.

The first half of the 20th century was the golden age of plant collecting. Britain already had a long history of exploring the world and studying the natural history of foreign countries. In the 18th and 19th centuries, British Naval vessels often had a naturalist onboard, the most famous probably being Charles Darwin. The Mutiny on the Bounty was triggered in part by the care given to the shipment of breadfruits in preference to the crew.

By about 1900, both North and South America had contributed a huge trove of plants to British Gardens and interest had turned to Asia. Much of the area was too tropical for its flora to survive in the English garden, but China had a more temperate climate and was ripe for exploration. In particular, the western province of Yunnan had an extraordinary biodiversity of new species and a climate similar to the milder parts of Britain, so it was very tempting to keen gardeners. The practice

was for a group of enthusiasts to fund the expedition of a plant-collector in return for a share of the seeds and plants brought back.

In 1925, Henry McLaren funded an expedition to Chile and Argentina by the Scottish botanist Harold Comber. In 1929, McLaren set up a syndicate for an expedition to Yunnan by another Scottish botanist, George Forrest. Henry bought two shares for £100 - about $6,500 today. Forrest was already famous and had been exploring and collecting in Yunnan since 1905. He received several awards from the Royal Horticultural Society and the Linnean society for his work. Yunnan was especially known for Rhododendrons, and the gardens at Bodnant had the mild climate and acid soil ideal for their cultivation. One of Forrest's collections was named after McLaren - Rhododendron aberconwayi.

Henry McLaren was responsible for much of the form of the gardens at Bodnant, especially the five terraces looking across to Snowdonia. In 1949, he gave the gardens to the National Trust but retained the house where he continued to live. Because of his horticultural reputation he also retained management of the gardens, an unusual arrangement for National Trust properties which continues today.

When Henry died in 1953, his son Charles became the 3rd Baron Aberconway and continued both the industrialist and horticultural traditions of his family. He became President of the Royal Horticultural Society, as his father had been before him. The garden continued in a traditional manner, with even the head-gardener, Mr. Puddle, coming from the same family for three generations.

The 3rd Baron died in 2003 and Bodnant passed to his second son Michael, also a barrister. He continues to live in the house at Bodnant and manage the gardens on behalf of the National Trust.

The Gardens

Bodnant has many parts to it, but there are two main sections. The five upper terraces are part of the more formal elements of the garden, and the Dell and other wooded areas contain the famous collections of trees and shrubs. The gardens have been extensively renovated by Michael McLaren and his head-gardener Troy Scott Smith, with a full-time staff of 21 gardeners, plus trainees and volunteers.

The East Lawn has beds of perennial flowering plants, as do the terraces, which are in a formal Italianate style, with ponds and fountains. The uppermost Rose Terrace has been renovated with a greater emphasis on color and flowers, as has the Lily Terrace and the Round Garden. The Laburnum Arch is a long, curving walkway enclosed in a metal archway covered in Laburnum trees, which is festooned with hanging clusters of yellow flowers in June. Pergola Walkways connect the terrace and the Rose Garden, which is at its height in June and July.

A building known as the Pin Mill stands at the end of a long, rectangular Pond which is covered in water lilies in summer. This building dates from 1730 and had indeed been a factory making pins. It was re-assembled at Bodnant in the 1930's from its original site in Gloucestershire. Another building, the Old Mill, was also erected at the bottom of the garden in the 1930's.

In May, the gardens are in full bloom with their famous Rhododendrons, Azaleas, Camellias and Magnolias. These can be seen in several areas of the garden, but most especially in The Dell, which was Henry Davis Pochin's original creation and still contains enormous specimens of Douglas Fir, California Redwoods and Sequoia he planted,

that are now over 150 feet tall. Other notable trees include the Dawn Redwood and the Handkerchief Tree (Davidia involucrata), both from China. From the Chilean expedition is the Chilean Fire bush (Embothrium lanceolatum) and Chilean Lantern Tree (Crinodendron hookerianum), both flowering in late May and June.

Further Reading

- The garden at Bodnant: the residence of Lord and Lady Aberconway, Jarrold Publishing (1997) – this book is also found in numerous other versions and editions.
- Road to Bodnant: The Story Behind the Famous North Wales Garden, by H.T. Milliken (1976)
- The gardens are also described in several general books on gardens in Wales and Britain.
- A recent biography of George Forrest, including information on his expedition for McLaren, is George Forrest: Plant Hunter, by Brenda McLean (2009)

Practical Information

The address of the Garden is Tal-y-Cafn, near Colwyn Bay, Conwy, Wales. It is near Snowdonia National Park (which can be seen from the garden). The town of Llandudno in Wales is nearby, and the garden is 65 miles from Liverpool.

The gardens are open every day of the year except for the 24th, 25th, and 26th of December. Opening hours are from 10 a.m. to 5 p.m. March to October and from 10 a.m. to 4 p.m. November to January.

The larger Bodnant Estate has several renovated cottages and farmhouses that can be rented for holidays and give access to the gardens, surrounding countryside and a lodge in Snowdonia Park.

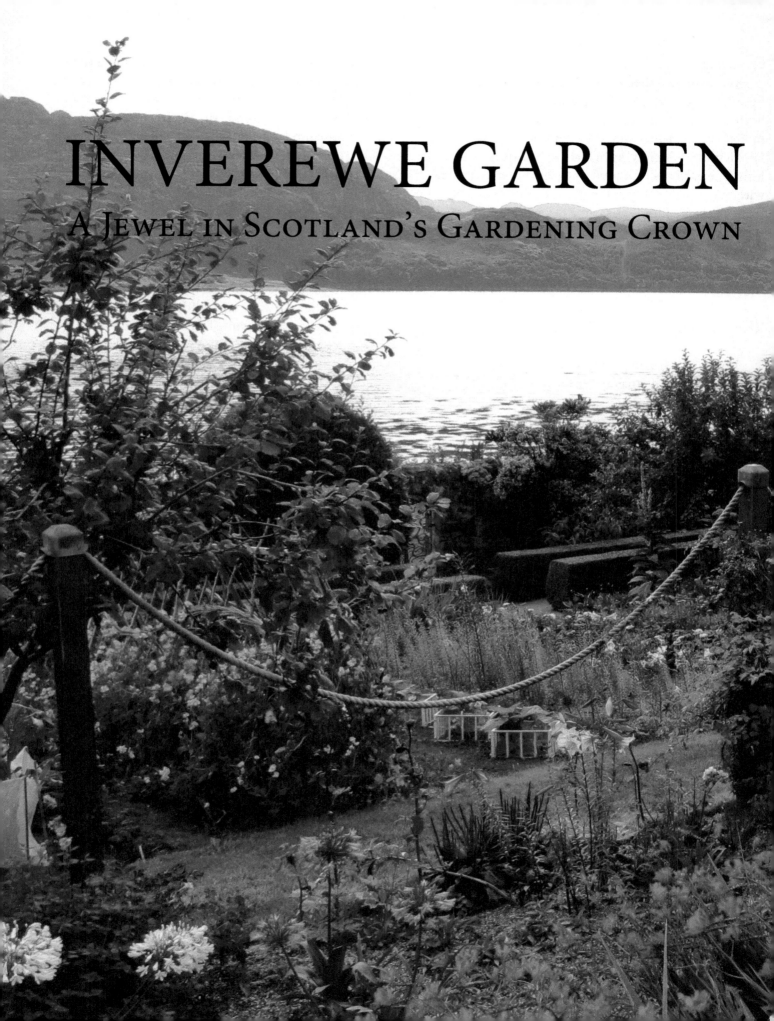

INVEREWE GARDEN

A Jewel in Scotland's Gardening Crown

Inverewe Garden, in northwest Scotland, is an unlikely collection of botanical marvels from around the world, growing in a sheltered garden that is warmed by the Gulf Stream. It was developed in the second-half of the 19th century and the early 20th century by Osgood Hanbury Mackenzie, who turned a barren, wind-swept rocky peninsula into a word-class garden with decades of steady work. The gardens were continued and further established by his daughter and are currently run by the National Trust for Scotland.

The Story

To a visitor, Scotland is perhaps the last place one would think of going to see subtropical plants, yet because the Gulf Stream strikes the west coast of Scotland directly, there are pockets with some of the mildest climates in the United Kingdom. Loch Ewe, in Wester Ross, in the far northwest, is such a place and it is home to the most spectacular garden in Scotland – Inverewe.

The Mackenzie Clan dates back to the 15th century, when Hector Roy Mackenzie was granted control of Gairloch, a tract of land in northwest Scotland.. The Scots have a long-standing close relationship with the French dating back to 1295, called the Auld Alliance, with Scotland and France sharing a common goal in reducing British expansionism. So the birth in 1842 of Osgood Hanbury Mackenzie at Chateau de Talhouet, near Quimperlé, in Brittany was not as odd as it may at first appear. Osgood's mother was born Mary Hanbury and may have been a distant relative of Thomas Hanbury, the founder of the famous Hanbury Gardens in Italy.

Osgood Mackenzie grew up in Brittany, his father having died a year after his birth, and he was educated at home, speaking both English and Gaelic. In the traditional manner, Osgood's older brother had inherited the vast Gairloch estate, so his choices for life seemed to be limited to the standard ones for a younger son, of the military or the church. However, Osgood made a different choice and in 1862, just 20 years old and with financial help from his mother, he purchased the 2,000 acre Inverewe Estate next door to Gairloch. While the area, further north than St. Petersburg in Russia, is warmed by the Gulf Stream, it is also buffeted by Atlantic storms and it was a barren, rocky place when the

young Mackenzie arrived. He built a mansion in the Scottish Baronial style and settled in to Highland life.

Perversely, Mackenzie chose a 50 acres peninsula pushing into the loch to create a garden. This piece of land, called Am Ploc Ard, or "the high lump", had one three-foot tall dwarf willow growing on it, most of the soil had been removed by crofters for their peat fires and it was infested with rabbits. Wisely Mackenzie realized he needed some shelter from the fierce winds, so he planted 100 acres surrounding the peninsula with thousands of trees, mostly pines, to create a shelter-belt.

Patience would seem to be a Mackenzie virtue, since now there was not much to do but wait for the trees to grow, which took about 20 years. To allow for some gardening he built a large walled garden, a popular Victorian method of providing shelter to grow vegetables and fruit.

Mackenzie, now 40, embarked on making a garden on Am Ploc Ard by planting into pockets of peat among the rocks in areas sheltered by the pine trees. This did not work well, so he hired a local man to carry baskets of better soil in on his back. It seems that in the end, he also imported soil from Ireland.

Gradually the garden began to take shape.

Unfortunately for garden historians, although Mackenzie wrote a volume of memoirs of his life at Inverewe, he devoted very little of it to his gardening, so we have only a general idea of how the garden was developed.

Mackenzie had married Minna Amy in 1877. She was the daughter of the 1st Baronet of Edwards-Moss, a large area of Lancashire. The couple had just one child, a daughter called Mairi Thyra, who was born in 1879. Osgood's marriage became troubled when Mairi was still a child, leading to a court dispute over custody between the estranged parents.

When Osgood Mackenzie died in 1922, Mairi inherited the property and with her first husband, a cousin named Robert Hanbury who she had married in 1907, she continued to care for the property and the garden. Robert Hanbury died in 1933 and Mairi remarried a local landowner and farmer, Ronald Sawyer.

The original mansion house had been almost destroyed by fire in 1914, and the families had been living in the Lodge House, another property on the estate, but Mairi and Ronald Sawyer now rebuilt the mansion and completed her father's dream for

the garden. Ronald died in 1945 and in 1952, with no children and approaching death, Mairi left the property to the National Trust for Scotland, along with an endowment for its upkeep.

At first, the remoteness of the area deterred visitors and only 3,000 people a year saw the gardens in those early years. This has gradually risen to 200,000 visits a year and the gardens are world-famous for the plant collections and the natural beauty of the location. The 2,000 acres of the estate surrounding the garden are a conservation area protecting many animals and birds, and the area is accessible to visitors through a series of walking trails. Those who drive to Inverewe from Inverness will also pass through some of the most spectacular scenery in Scotland.

The Gardens

The late nineteenth century was the era of the great plant-hunters who brought new discoveries from around the world to England, establishing its reputation as a centre of gardening innovation. Mackenzie used many of these new plants in his garden, drawing from Australia and New Zealand, South Africa, South America and China to build the core of a collection of 25,000 species and varieties of plants, including many rarities found normally only much further south.

A highlight of the garden is a series of terraces known as South Africa. As the name suggests, the landscape here is a recreation of the natural beauty of the Cape Province and the Drakensberg Mountains. Most of the plants have been grown at the gardens from seed collected in the wild or from plants imported from the world-famous gardens at Kirstenbosch - South Africa's national botanical garden.

The original Walled Garden is still dominated by vegetables, grown organically. The beds are mulched and enriched in winter with seaweed blown up onto the beach from the Loch by the gales that buffet the area in fall.

The Woods adjacent to the garden contain many rare and exotic trees including the world's most northerly planting of rare Wollemi pines (Wollemia nobilis) from Australia, which are not true pines, but are critically endangered in their natural habitat. There are numerous Eucalyptus from Australia and New Zealand as well as rhododendrons from China, Nepal and India. The Himalayan Blue Poppy (Meconopsis grandis) thrives in the peaty, moist woodland.

Walking Trails through the estate reveal many wildflowers, as well as Red Deer, White-tailed Eagles. Ospreys and other wild-life.

Further Reading

- A Hundred Years in the Highlands by Osgood Hanbury Mackenzie (edit M. T. Sawyer)
- Eighty Years in the Highlands: The Life and Times of Osgood Mackenzie of Inverewe by Pauline Butler
- Inverewe: an Illustrated Guide To Inverewe Garden by Mairi T. Sawyer
- Inverewe: a Garden in the North-West Highlands by May Cowan
- Inverewe by Peter Clough

Practical Information

The address of the Garden is Inverewe Garden, Poolewe, Ross, and Cromarty, Scotland.

The gardens are open from late March to the end of October, every day of the week. Entrance is between 10am and 5 or 6pm. During this period, there is also a restaurant and gift shop at the gardens. During the winter months, the gardens only are open, from 10am to3 pm.

Visitors who plan to also walk in the conservation area are advised to bring insect repellent and waterproof walking boots.

It is also possible to stay in the Lodge House, giving 24-hour access to the gardens and a base for visiting Scotland.

LEVENS HALL

AN ICONIC DUTCH STYLE TOPIARY GARDEN

Levens Hall, in Cumbria, is one of a very few remaining examples of the Dutch Style of Topiary, popular towards the end of the 17th century. As well as over 100 clipped trees, each one in a different shape, the garden has beautiful herbaceous borders and examples of other gardening styles appropriate to the age of the gardens. The house is a rare Elizabethan mansion, and this is the gateway to the Lake District, one of the most beautiful natural areas of England.

The Story

The border between England and Scotland has had a troubled history of warfare and battles. In the 13th century, fortified houses were common, and it was during that time that the first building took place at Levens. During the more peaceful Elizabethan period, the Bellingham family purchased the medieval fortified towers and in 1562, converted it into a larger and more comfortable Elizabethan mansion, which still stands today. In 1688, the property was sold to Colonel James Grahme to settle gambling debts that the Bellingham of the time had accumulated.

Colonel Grahme had been 'Keeper of the Privy Purse' and 'Master of the King's Buckhounds' at the court of King James II, but with the 'Glorious Revolution' of that year, Colonel Grahme was out of favor at the new court of William & Mary, so he retreated to Levens Hall to bide his time. He took with him James's gardener, the Frenchman Monsieur Guillaume Beaumont, who had been built some of the gardens at Hampton Court Palace.

The house was expanded, and Beaumont constructed a garden in the then fashionable Dutch style, perhaps in recognition of the new King's background. This style was derived from the grand formal Renaissance gardens of Europe, especially France, which had been constructed with long, straight grass pathways flanked with trees, often clipped flat to a considerable height. The second important feature was the parterre (literally 'divided earth'), made up of low clipped hedges making ornate patterns on the ground, with different colored gravels and later plants, filling the spaces in between.

When the taste for this formalism arrived in the Netherlands, the small spaces available made French-style gardens impossible, so the Dutch

la
"enco
splendi
facile com
shapeless po
    Colonel Gra
his name to Graha
of parliament, despit
secret Roman Catholic.

clipped up instead of across, making the hedges themselves the ornamentation and creating elaborately shaped forms with clipped plants. This Dutch Style proved popular in England too, where again, space was often at a premium. This art of clipping plants into shapes was known as 'topiary', from the French topiaire, which in turn came from the Latin word for a landscape gardener – topiaries.

Tastes in gardening change with the times, and by one of those historical coincidences, the man who would bring about the next change, the poet Alexander Pope, was born in 1688, the year Grahme purchased Levens Hall. Pope's gardening disciples, William Kent and Capability Brown, developed the English Landscape Style of gardening. In the words of the famous British 20th-century landscape designer Russell Page, Brown was busy encouraging his wealthy clients to tear out their formal gardens and replace them with his compositions of grass, tree clumps and rather pools and lakes".

Grahme had a son, Henry, who changed his name and became a Tory member allegations that he was a He married an illegitimate daughter of King Charles II, which created such as scandal that he lost his position at the court of Queen Anne's husband, Prince George of Denmark, the Duke of Cumberland.

Colonel Grahme's daughter, Catherine, married Henry Bowes Howard, 4th Earl of Berkshire and when the Colonel died in 1730, the estate passed to her. Henry Howard had several more important estates, meaning that Levens Hall received little attention and the gardens escaped the style changes going on around them. This continued after his death when Catherine refused a series of requests to take down the garden and turn it into grazing land for sheep.

In 1803 the estate passed, via another female heir, to the Bagot family, a family of Barons going back to the 11th century. Today Levens Hall is occupied by a 'junior branch' of the Bagot family, Charles (Hal) and Susie Bagot. They have extended and developed the gardens, adding new features but preserving the original topiary gardens. By the vagaries of history, Levens Hall is one of the very few remaining examples of this style, and certainly the most prominent one.

The Gardens

The chief feature of the gardens is, of course, the topiary trees. There are over 100 pieces, each clipped in a unique shape. It takes from late August to early January for all of the pieces to receive their annual clipping. The garden is managed by Chris Crowder, only the tenth head gardener on the property since the 1690s when the gardens were laid out by Beaumont. The gardens are maintained by a team of five part-time gardeners, with the assistance of volunteers and international interns.

The Topiary Gardens are in the front of the house, and some of the pieces are original – over three hundred years old. The pieces are made of Yew or Boxwood. Most are abstract, but some represent chess pieces, peacocks, lions or Queen Elizabeth and her Maids of Honor. The topiary is placed in a parterre, which is planted seasonally with annual flowers and bulbs using over 15,000 plants twice a year.

The double-sided Herbaceous Borders run across the property and contain a wide variety of perennial plants, supplemented in summer with annual flowers and plants.

The Rose Garden is planted entirely with a type of rose developed by the rose breeder, David Austin, from hybrids between modern, repeat-flowering roses and 'antique' roses, giving more-or-less continuous flowering in a rose with an old-fashioned form.

There is an Orchard with ancient apple trees covered in blossom in the spring, along with quinces and plums, all set in grass dotted with tulips and wildflowers.

There is also a formal Herb Garden and a recently added 17th Century Garden behind the house.

Practical Information

The address of the Garden is Levens Hall, Kendal, Cumbria.

The gardens are open from early April to early October, from Sundays to Thursdays (closed on Fridays and Saturdays). The gardens open from 10 am – 5 pm and the house from noon to 4:30 pm.

Printed in the USA
CPSIA information can be obtained
at www.ICGtesting.com
LVHW072321060124
768328LV00018B/1478